VAN GOGH

A POSTCARD BOOK™

Running Press • Philadelphia, Pennsylvania

Postcard Book is a trademark of Running Press Book Publishers.

Canadian representatives: General Publishing Co., Ltd., 30 Lesmill Road, Don Mills, Ontario M3B 2T6. International representatives: Worldwide Media Services, Inc., 115 East Twenty-third Street, New York, NY 10010.

9   8   7   6   5   4   3   2   1
The digit on the right indicates the number of this printing.

ISBN 0-89471-648-4

Cover design by Toby Schmidt.
Cover illustration: *Self-Portrait in Front of the Easel,* 1888, by Vincent van Gogh. Rijksmuseum Vincent van Gogh, Amsterdam. (The Granger Collection, New York)
Back cover illustration: *Starry Night,* 1889, by Vincent van Gogh. Museum of Modern Art, New York. (The Granger Collection, New York) Title page illustration: *The Red Vineyard,* 1888, by Vincent van Gogh. Pushkin Museum, Moscow. (Kavaler/Art Resource, New York)
Typography by TypeMasters, Inc., West Conshohocken, PA.
Printed and bound in the United States of America.
This book may be ordered by mail from the publisher. Please include $1.50 postage. *But try your bookstore first!* Running Press Book Publishers, 125 South Twenty-second Street, Philadelphia, Pennsylvania 19103.

Vincent van Gogh sold only one painting in his lifetime. That painting, *Red Vineyard,* was purchased four months before the artist's death in 1890, for about $80. Less than 100 years later, van Gogh's *Irises* set a world record for the sale of a single painting when it was auctioned for nearly $54 million. In his lifetime, van Gogh was considered a misfit and a failure. Today he is recognized as a visionary who helped shape modern art.

Van Gogh didn't set out to be a painter. The intensity and zeal that are so evident in his paintings he first tried to channel in other directions—as a preacher, as an art dealer, as a schoolteacher—all of which proved calamitous.

At age 27 he decided to be an artist. Although he attended classes, he had no patience for them. He preferred painting from life rather than from the plaster models his teacher relied upon, and he learned by studying the work of masters such as his countryman, Rembrandt, and later by moving to Paris to learn the techniques of Toulouse-Lautrec, Gauguin, and other young artists.

His first works pictured the fields and laborers of Holland. His somber palette and unromantic portrayal of these subjects, typified by *The Potato Eaters,* made these paintings unsalable.

In 1886, van Gogh moved to Paris, and as the artistic renaissance underway there exerted its influence on him, he began to choose lighter colors and brighter themes. His sumptuous use of color reached its peak in Arles, where he moved in 1888. In the brilliant sun of the south of France, van Gogh painted his most energetic, luminous, and now-famous works. Just as he was on the verge of recognition as an artist, he suffered a series of violent mental episodes and committed suicide in 1890.

During the 10 years that van Gogh struggled for self-expression through his art, his brother Theo remained his constant—and often his only—source of spiritual and financial support. Their correspondence is testimony to the bond the brothers shared, and offers a remarkable glimpse of the world through the eyes of the artist.

In a letter to Theo in 1882, Vincent wrote,

> "...I want to reach so far that people will say of my work: he feels deeply, he feels tenderly—notwithstanding my so-called roughness, perhaps even because of this....It is true that I am often in the greatest misery, but still there is within me a calm pure harmony and music."

Only later did others begin to hear the music he heard; and it is brave, and tragic, and beautiful.

VASE WITH PEONIES AND ROSES

1886, by Vincent van Gogh (Dutch, 1853–1890). Oil on canvas. Rijksmuseum Kröller-Müller, Otterlo, Netherlands. (The Granger Collection, New York)

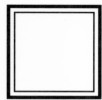

A PAIR OF SHOES

1886, by Vincent van Gogh (Dutch, 1853–1890). Oil on canvas. Rijksmuseum
Vincent van Gogh, Amsterdam. (The Granger Collection, New York)

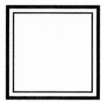

SELF-PORTRAIT WITH STRAW HAT

1887, by Vincent van Gogh (Dutch, 1853–1890). Oil on canvas. Metropolitan Museum of Art, New York. (The Granger Collection, New York)

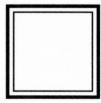

VAN GOGH A Postcard Book™ © 1988 by Running Press Book Publishers

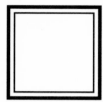

SELF-PORTRAIT IN FRONT OF THE EASEL

1888, by Vincent van Gogh (Dutch, 1853–1890). Oil on canvas. Rijksmuseum
Vincent van Gogh, Amsterdam. (The Granger Collection, New York)

THE DRAWBRIDGE NEAR ARLES

1888, by Vincent van Gogh (Dutch, 1853–1890). Oil on canvas. Rijksmuseum Kröller-Müller, Otterlo, Netherlands. (The Granger Collection, New York)

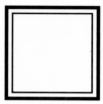

PEACH TREES IN BLOSSOM (SOUVENIR DE MAUVE)

1888, by Vincent van Gogh (Dutch, 1853–1890). Oil on canvas. Rijksmuseum Kröller-Müller, Otterlo, Netherlands. (The Granger Collection, New York)

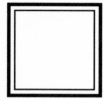

HAYSTACKS IN PROVENCE

1888, by Vincent van Gogh (Dutch, 1853–1890). Oil on canvas. Rijksmuseum Kröller-Müller, Otterlo, Netherlands. (The Granger Collection, New York)

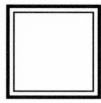

FISHING BOATS ON THE BEACH AT SAINTES-MARIES

1888, by Vincent van Gogh (Dutch, 1853–1890). Oil on canvas. Rijksmuseum
Vincent van Gogh, Amsterdam. (The Granger Collection, New York)

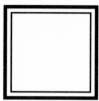

THE NIGHT CAFÉ

1888, by Vincent van Gogh (Dutch, 1853–1890). Oil on canvas. Yale University Art Gallery, New Haven, Connecticut. (The Granger Collection, New York)

CAFÉ TERRACE AT NIGHT

1888, by Vincent van Gogh (Dutch, 1853–1890). Oil on canvas. Rijksmuseum Kröller-Müller, Otterlo, Netherlands. (The Granger Collection, New York)

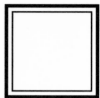

VAN GOGH A Postcard Book™ © 1988 by Running Press Book Publishers

THE ALYSCAMPS

1888, by Vincent van Gogh (Dutch, 1853–1890). Oil on canvas. Rijksmuseum Kröller-Müller, Otterlo, Netherlands. (The Granger Collection, New York)

THE ARLÉSIENNE (MADAME GINOUX)

1888, by Vincent van Gogh (Dutch, 1853–1890). Oil on canvas. Musée d'Orsay, Paris. (The Granger Collection, New York)

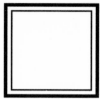

THE RED VINEYARD

1888, by Vincent van Gogh (Dutch, 1853–1890). Oil on canvas. Pushkin Museum, Moscow. (Kavaler/Art Resource, New York)

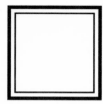

THE SOWER

1888, by Vincent van Gogh (Dutch, 1853–1890). Oil on canvas. Rijksmuseum Vincent van Gogh, Amsterdam. (The Granger Collection, New York)

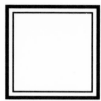

THE DANCE HALL

1888, by Vincent van Gogh (Dutch, 1853–1890). Oil on canvas. Musée d'Orsay, Paris. (Kavaler/Art Resource, New York)

VAN GOGH A Postcard Book™   © 1988 by Running Press Book Publishers

DRAWING BOARD WITH ONIONS

1889, by Vincent van Gogh (Dutch, 1853–1890). Oil on canvas. Rijksmuseum
Kröller-Müller, Otterlo, Netherlands. (The Granger Collection, New York)

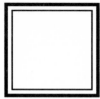

SUNFLOWERS IN A VASE

1889, by Vincent van Gogh (Dutch, 1853–1890). Oil on canvas. Rijksmuseum
Vincent van Gogh, Amsterdam. (The Granger Collection, New York)

L A BERCEUSE (MADAME ROULIN)

1889, by Vincent van Gogh (Dutch, 1853–1890). Oil on canvas. Rijksmuseum Kröller-Müller, Otterlo, Netherlands. (The Granger Collection, New York)

VAN GOGH A Postcard Book™   © 1988 by Running Press Book Publishers

THE POSTMAN ROULIN

1889, by Vincent van Gogh (Dutch, 1853–1890). Oil on canvas. Rijksmuseum Kröller-Müller, Otterlo, Netherlands. (The Granger Collection, New York)

HARVEST TIME

1889, by Vincent van Gogh (Dutch, 1853–1890). Oil on canvas. Folkwang
Museum, Essen, West Germany. (Giraudon/Art Resource, New York)

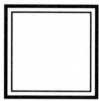

VAN GOGH A Postcard Book™ © 1988 by Running Press Book Publishers

STARRY NIGHT

1889, by Vincent van Gogh (Dutch, 1853–1890). Oil on canvas. Museum of Modern Art, New York. (The Granger Collection, New York)

VAN GOGH A Postcard Book™   © 1988 by Running Press Book Publishers

EVENING WALK

1889, by Vincent van Gogh (Dutch, 1853–1890). Oil on canvas. Museu de Arte, São Paulo, Brazil. (Giraudon/Art Resource, New York)

GREEN WHEAT

1889, by Vincent van Gogh (Dutch, 1853–1890). Oil on canvas. Národní Galerie, Prague. (Art Resource, New York)

THE FIELDS

1890, by Vincent van Gogh (Dutch, 1853–1890). Oil on canvas. Private collection.
(Giraudon/Art Resource, New York)

THE MEADOW WITH BUTTERFLIES (ASYLUM GARDEN)

1890, by Vincent van Gogh (Dutch, 1853–1890). Oil on canvas. National Gallery, London. (The Granger Collection, New York)

VAN GOGH A Postcard Book™ © 1988 by Running Press Book Publishers

VASE WITH IRISES

1890, by Vincent van Gogh (Dutch, 1853–1890). Oil on canvas. Rijksmuseum
Vincent van Gogh, Amsterdam. (The Granger Collection, New York)

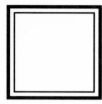

VAN GOGH A Postcard Book™   © 1988 by Running Press Book Publishers

ROAD WITH CYPRESS AND STAR

1890, by Vincent van Gogh (Dutch, 1853–1890). Oil on canvas. Rijksmuseum
Kröller-Müller, Otterlo, Netherlands. (The Granger Collection, New York)

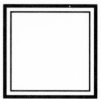

VAN GOGH A Postcard Book™   © 1988 by Running Press Book Publishers

COTTAGES WITH THATCHED ROOFS

1890, by Vincent van Gogh (Dutch, 1853–1890). Oil on canvas. Louvre, Paris.
(The Granger Collection, New York)

THE CHURCH AT AUVERS

1890, by Vincent van Gogh (Dutch, 1853–1890). Oil on canvas. Musée d'Orsay, Paris. (The Granger Collection, New York)

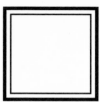

LANDSCAPE WITH CARRIAGE AND TRAIN IN THE DISTANCE

1890, by Vincent van Gogh (Dutch, 1853–1890). Oil on canvas. Pushkin Museum, Moscow. (Kavaler/Art Resource, New York)

$6.95

"What would life be if we had no courage to attempt anything
— Vincent van Go

Running Press
Book Publishers

ISBN 0-89471-6